FastTrack
MUSIC INSTRUCTION

Harmonica 2
Songbook

ISBN 978-0-634-09646-4

HAL•LEONARD®
CORPORATION

7777 W. BLUEMOUND RD. P.O. BOX 13819 MILWAUKEE, WI 53213

Visit Hal Leonard online at **www.halleonard.com**

INTRODUCTION

Welcome back to FastTrack®

We hope you enjoyed Harmonica 2 and are ready to play some hits. Have you and your friends formed a band? Or do you feel like soloing along with the CD? Either way, make sure you're relaxed... it's time to jam!

The eight songs in this book are in the keys of the originals. You can still play them with your C diatonic harmonica, but you won't be able to play along with the CD unless you get a diatonic harmonica in the key of the song. The key of the harmonica and position to be played is found at the beginning of each song.

This songbook further differs from the FastTrack® Harmonica 1 Songbook in that the emphasis is to give you more practice on draw bends and to play more melody instead of accompaniment.

As with Harmonica 2, don't try to bite off more than you can chew. If you're tired, take some time off. If you get frustrated, put down your harp, relax, and just listen to the CD, If you forget something, go back and relearn it. Always remember the three Ps: **patience**, **practice**, and **pace yourself**... and of course the fourth P: **pride**, for a job well done.

CONTENTS

CD Track	Song Title	Page
1	Bang a Gong (Get It On)	5
2	Cocaine	8
3	Knock on Wood	10
4	Let's Stay Together	13
5	Mustang Sally	16
6	No Particular Place to Go	20
7	Stuck in the Middle with You	23
8	Walk on By	27

ABOUT THE CD

Again, you get a CD with the book! Each song in the book is included on the CD, so you can hear how it sounds and play along when you're ready.

Each example on the CD is preceded by one measure of "clicks" to indicate the tempo and meter. Pan right to hear the harmonica part emphasized. Pan left to hear the accompaniment part emphasized.

Bang a Gong
(Get It On)
Words and Music by Marc Bolan

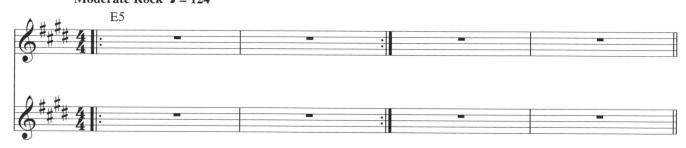

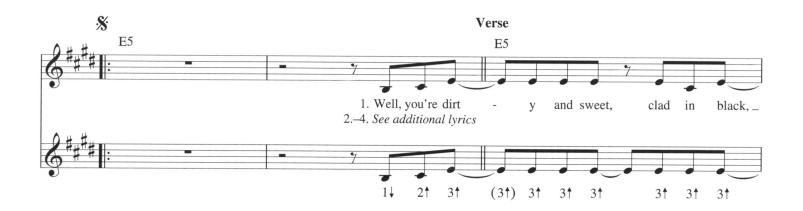

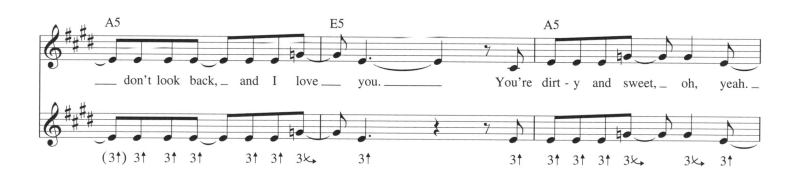

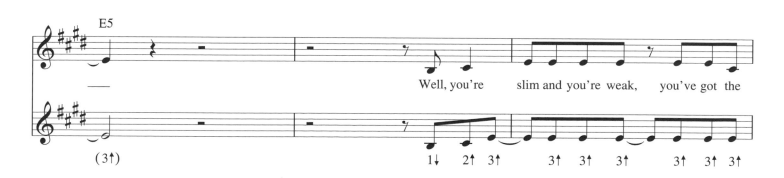

teeth of the hy - dra up - on_____ you._____ You're dirt - y, sweet, and you're my girl._

Chorus
To Coda ⊕

Get it on._____ Bang a gong._

Get it on. Get it on._

Bang a gong._ Get it on.

D.S. al Coda

Interlude

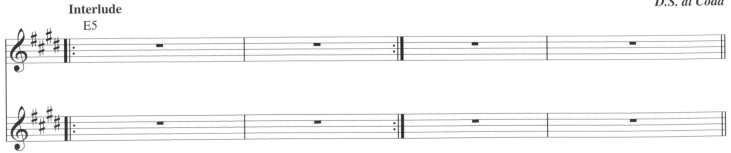

6

Coda

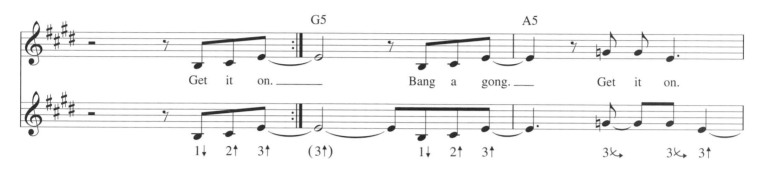

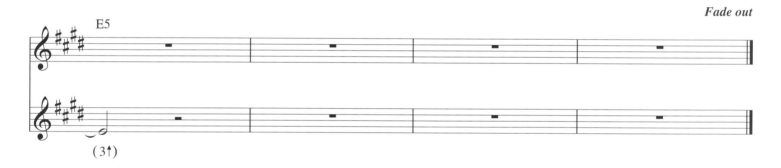

Additional Lyrics

2. Well, you're built like a car,
   You've got a hubcap diamond star halo.
   You're built like a car, oh, yeah.
   Well, you're an untamed youth, that's the truth,
   With your cloak full of eagles.
   You're dirty, sweet, and you're my girl.

3. Well, you're windy and wild,
   You've got the blues in your shoes and your stockings.
   You're windy and wild, oh, yeah.
   Well, you're built like a car,
   You've got a hubcap diamond star halo.
   You're dirty, sweet, and you're my girl.

4. Well, you're dirty and sweet,
   Clad in black, don't look back, and I love you.
   You're dirty and sweet, oh, yeah.
   Well, you dance when you walk,
   So let's dance, take a chance, understand me.
   You're dirty, sweet, and you're my girl.

❷ Cocaine

Words and Music by J.J. Cale

she don't lie, ____ she don't lie, ____ co - caine. ____

(3↖) 2↖ 2↓ 3↖   2↖ 2↓ 3↖   3↑ 3↑

|1. |2.

To Coda ⊕

E   D   E   D

2. If   you

6↑ 6↑

Guitar Solo   **D.S. al Coda**

E   D   E   D   E   D   D
Play 11 times

3. If   your

6↑ 6↑

⊕ **Coda**

She don't lie, ____ she don't lie, ____ she don't lie, ____   co - caine. _

2↖ 2↓ 3↖   2↖ 2↓ 3↖   2↖ 2↓ 3↖   3↑ 3↑

Repeat and fade

E   D   E   D   E   D   D

(Ad lib fills until fade)

(3↑)

❸ Knock on Wood

Words and Music by Eddie Floyd and Steve Cropper

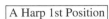

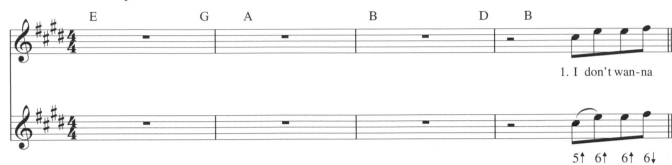

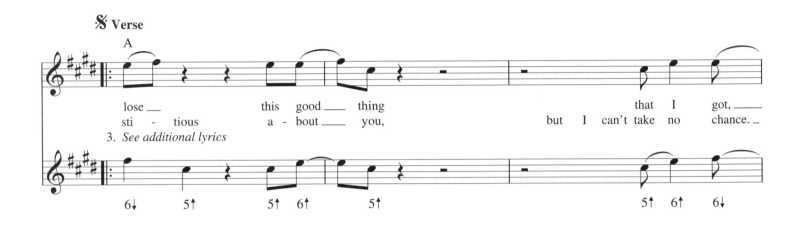

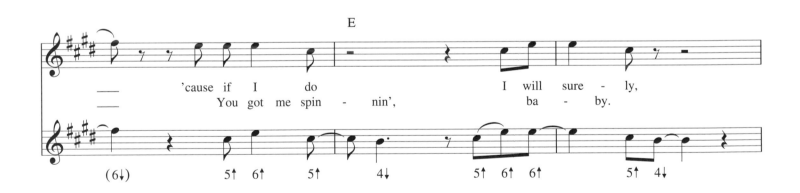

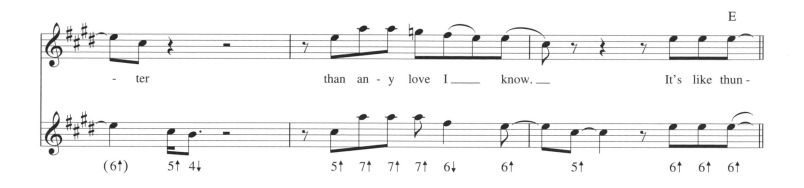

-ter   than an - y love I ____ know. ____   It's like thun-

(6↑) 5↑ 4↓   5↑ 7↑ 7↑ 7↑ 6↓   6↑   5↑   6↑ 6↑ 6↑

Chorus

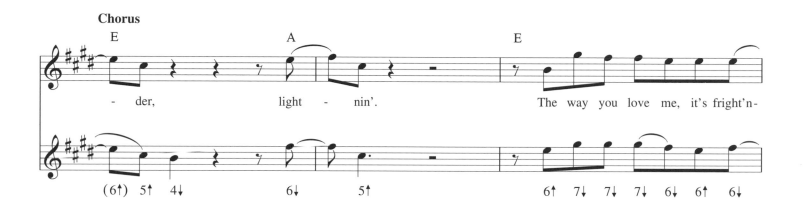

-der,   light - nin'.   The way you love me, it's fright'n-

(6↑) 5↑ 4↓   6↓   5↑   6↑ 7↓ 7↓ 7↓ 6↓ 6↑ 6↓

To Coda ⊕

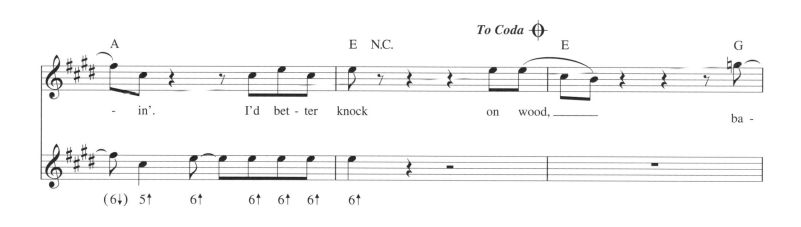

-in'.   I'd bet-ter knock   on wood, _____   ba-

(6↓) 5↑   6↑   6↑ 6↑ 6↑   6↑

1.

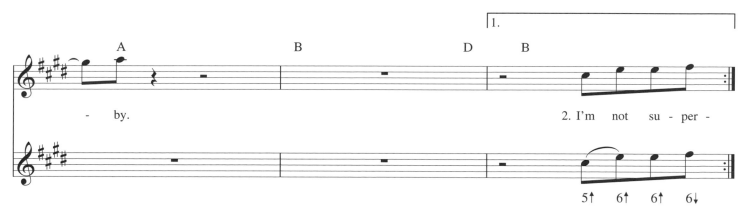

-by.   2. I'm not su-per-

5↑ 6↑ 6↑ 6↓

Additional Lyrics

3. Ain't no secret that woman
   Is my lovin' cup.
   Yes, she sees to it
   That I get enough.
   Just one touch from her,
   You know, it means so much.

◆ Let's Stay Together

Words and Music by Al Green, Willie Mitchell and Al Jackson, Jr.

F Harp 1st Position

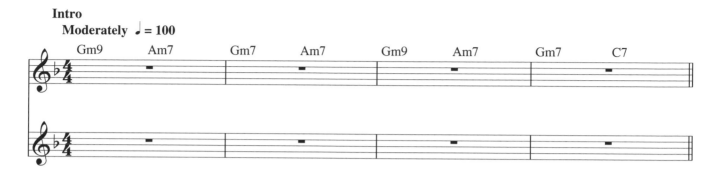

Intro
Moderately ♩ = 100

Verse

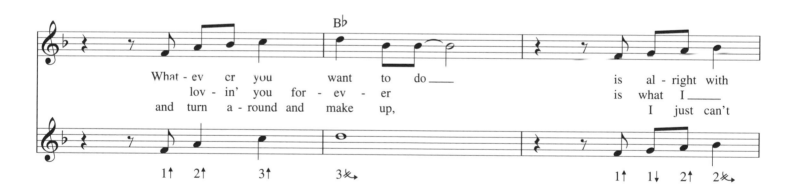

14

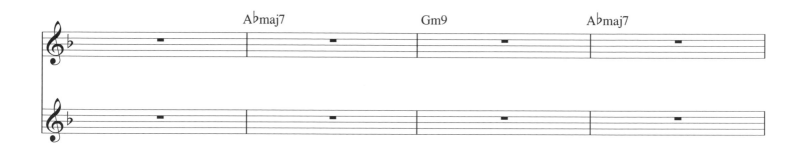

D.S. al Coda

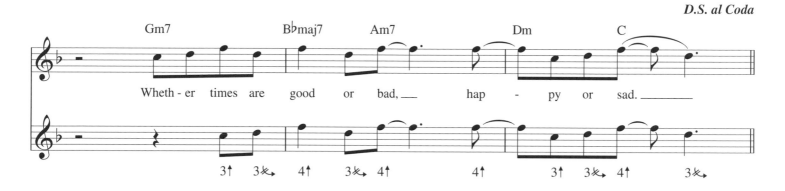

Wheth - er times are good or bad, ___ hap - py or sad. ___

3↑ 3↘ 4↑ 3↘ 4↑ 4↑ 3↑ 3↘ 4↑ 3↘

Coda

Outro

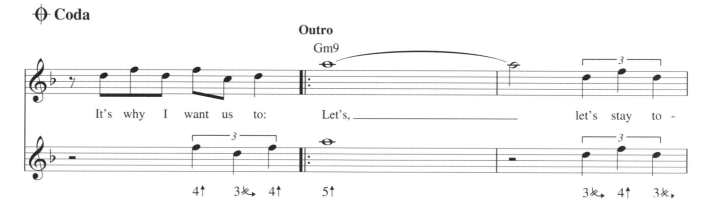

It's why I want us to: Let's, ___ let's stay to -

4↑ 3↘ 4↑ 5↑ 3↘ 4↑ 3↘

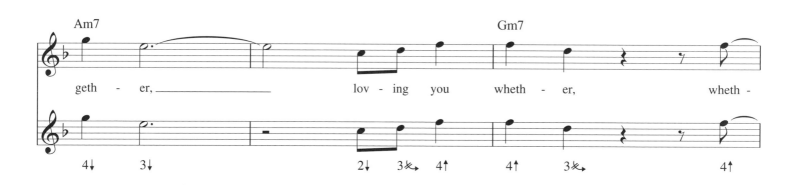

geth - er, ___ lov - ing you wheth - er, wheth -

4↓ 3↓ 2↓ 3↘ 4↑ 4↑ 3↘ 4↑

Repeat and fade

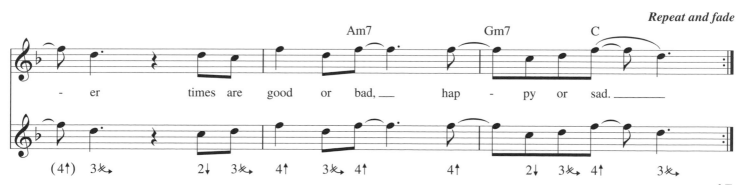

- er times are good or bad, ___ hap - py or sad. ___

(4↑) 3↘ 2↓ 3↘ 4↑ 3↘ 4↑ 4↑ 2↓ 3↘ 4↑ 3↘

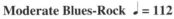
Mustang Sally

Words and Music by Bonny Rice

F Harp 2nd Position

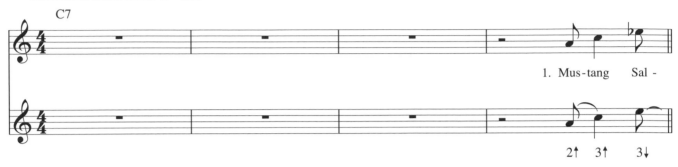

Intro
Moderate Blues-Rock ♩ = 112

1. Mus-tang Sal -

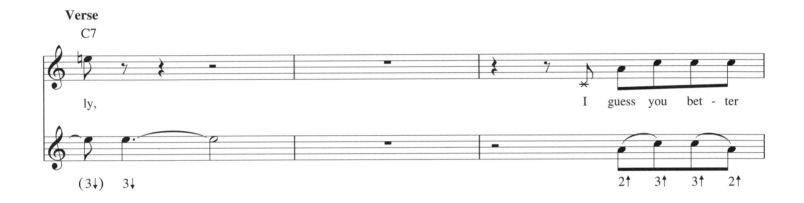

ly,

I guess you bet - ter

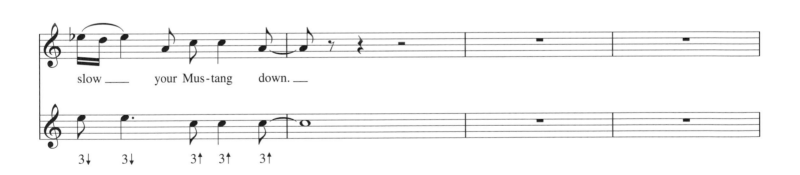

slow ___ your Mus-tang down. ___

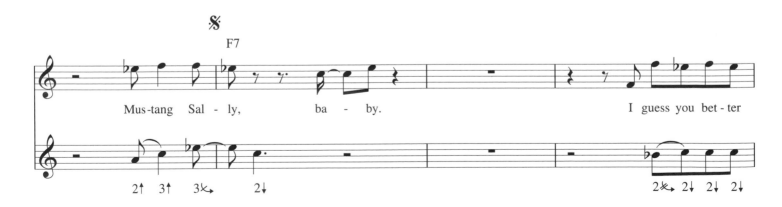

Mus-tang Sal - ly, ba - by.

I guess you bet - ter

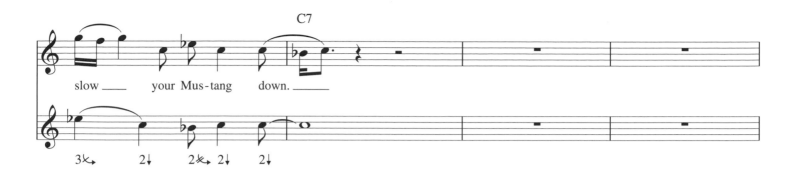

slow ___ your Mus-tang down. _____

3↘ 2↓ 2↘ 2↓ 2↓

G7   G♭7

You been run-nin' all   o - ver ___ town. _____
You've been go-in' a-round ___ all o-ver town. _____

3↘ 3↘   3↘ 3↘ 3↘ 3↘ 3↘   3↑ 2↘   1↓

F7   C7

Oo, you're gon-na have to put your flat feet ___ on _____ the ground. _
Oo, I'm gon-na have to put your big feet ___ on _____ the ground. _

4↑ 4↑ 4↑ 4↑ 4↑ 4↑   4↑ 4↑ 4↑ 3↘   2↓ 2↘   2↓

To Coda

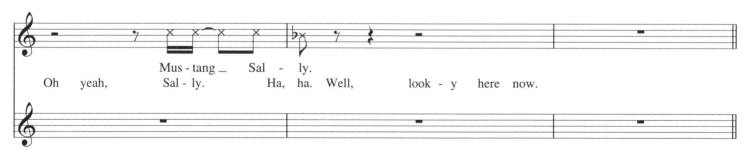

Mus-tang ___ Sal - ly. _

Oh   yeah,   Sal - ly.   Ha, ha. Well,   look - y here now.

Chorus

C7

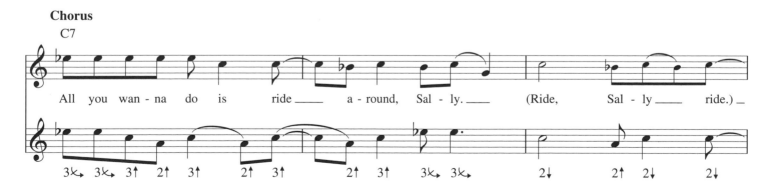

All you wan-na do is ride ___ a - round, Sal - ly. ___ (Ride, Sal - ly ___ ride.) _

3↘ 3↘ 3↑ 2↑ 3↑   2↑ 3↑   2↑ 3↑ 3↘ 3↘   2↓   2↑ 2↓ 2↓

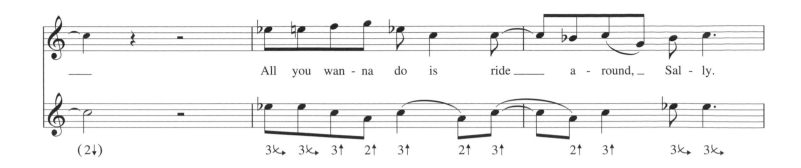

All you wan-na do is ride ___ a - round, ___ Sal - ly.

(2↓)   3↘ 3↘ 3↑ 2↑ 3↑   2↑ 3↑   2↑ 3↑   3↘ 3↘

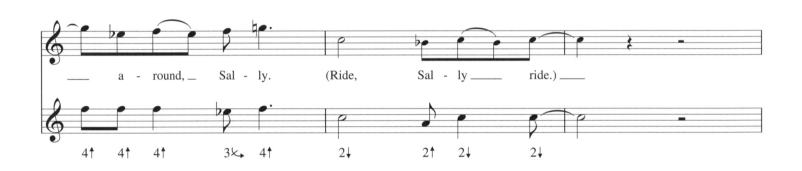

(Ride,   Sal - ly ___ ride.) ___   All you wan - na do is ride ___

2↓   2↑ 2↓   2↓   4↑ 4↑ 4↑ 4↑ 4↑ 3↘

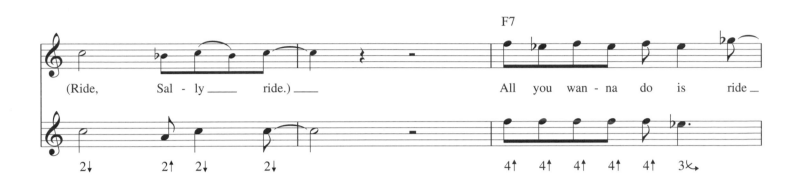

___ a - round, ___ Sal - ly.   (Ride,   Sal - ly ___ ride.) ___

4↑ 4↑ 4↑   3↘ 4↑   2↓   2↑ 2↓   2↓

F7

C7

All you wan-na do is ride ___ a - round, ___ Sal - ly.   (Ride,   Sal - ly ___ ride.) ___

3↘ 3↘ 3↑ 2↓ 3↑   2↓ 3↑   2↓ 3↑   3↘ 3↘   2↓   2↑ 2↓   2↓

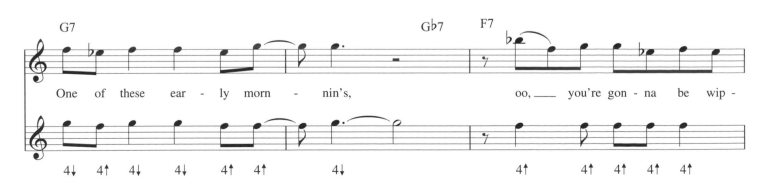

G7   Gb7   F7

One of these ear - ly morn - nin's,   oo, ___ you're gon - na be wip -

4↓ 4↑ 4↓   4↓   4↑ 4↑   4↓   4↑   4↑ 4↑ 4↑ 4↑

18

Verse

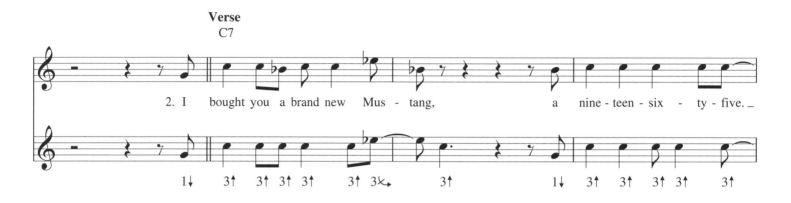

D.S. al Coda   Coda

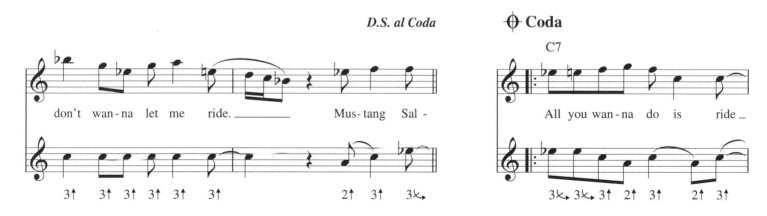

Repeat and fade

◆ No Particular Place to Go

Words and Music by Chuck Berry

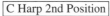

C Harp 2nd Position

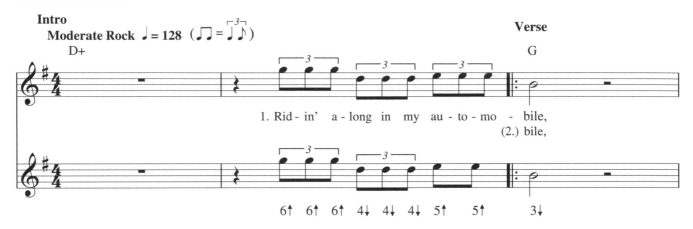

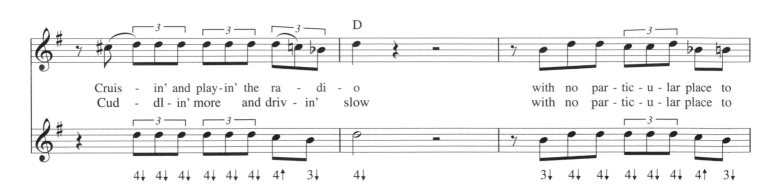

so we both de-cid-ed to take a stroll.
For the safe-ty belt that would-n't budge.
Can you i-mag-ine the way ‒ I
Cruis-in' and play-in' the rad - i -

3↑ 4↓ 4↓ 4↓ 4↓ 4↓ 4↓ 3↓   4↓ 4↓ 4↓ 4↓ 4↓ 4↓ 4↑ 3↓

felt?
o

I couldn't un - fas - ten her safe - ty belt.
With no par - tic - u - lar place to go.

4↓   3↓ 4↓ 4↓ 4↓ 4↓ 4↓ 4↑ 3↓ 3↑

1.   **2.**

Outro-Guitar Solo

4. Rid- in' a- long in my cal - a -

(optional harmonica solo)

6↑ 6↑ 6↑ 4↓ 4↓ 4↓ 5↑ 5↑

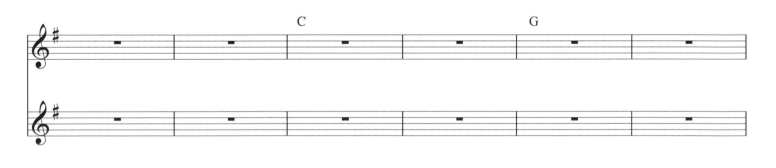

1.   **2.**

D   C   G   G   A♭7 G7

4↓ 4↓ 4↘ 4↘ 4↑ 4↑   3↓ 1↓ 2↑ 2↘   2↓
                              release

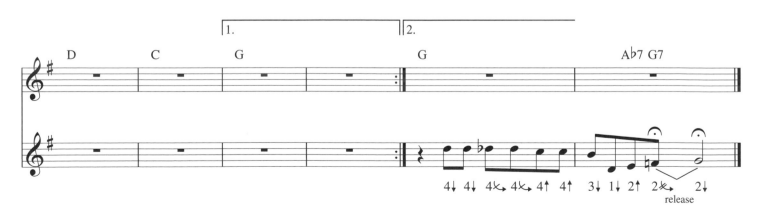

◆7 Stuck in the Middle with You

Words and Music by Gerry Rafferty and Joe Egan

C Harp 3rd Position

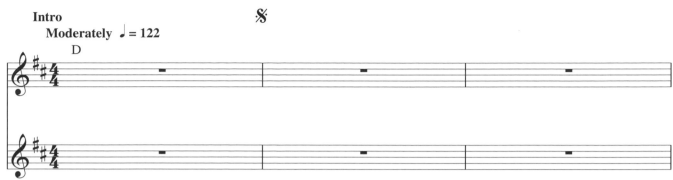

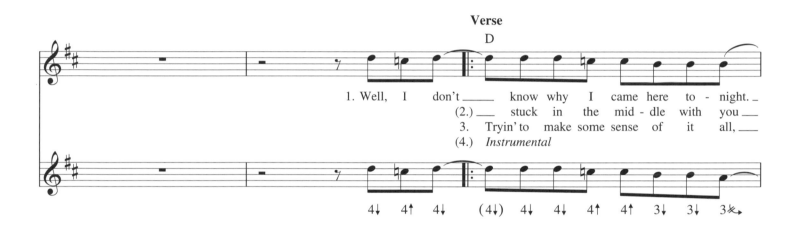

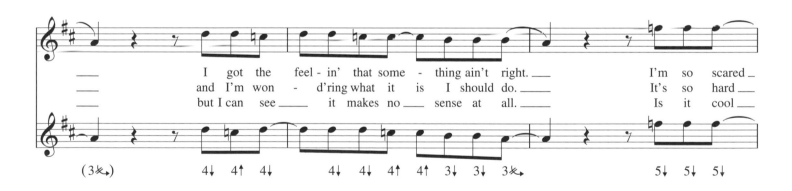

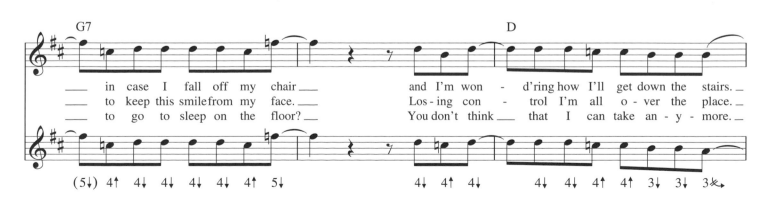

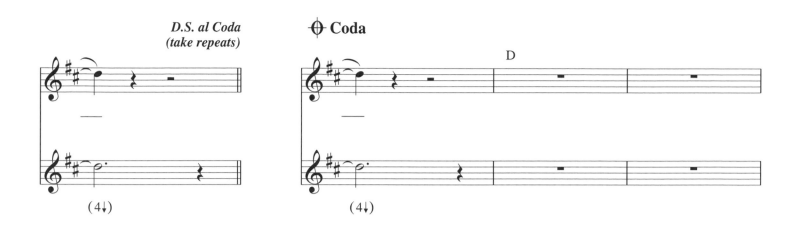

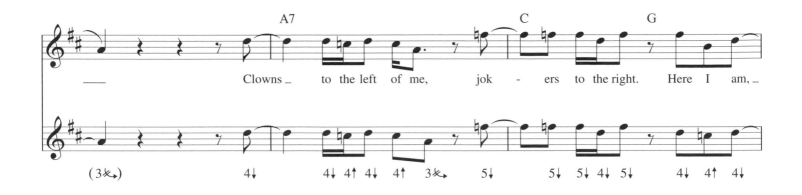

Outro

26

⬧⑧ Walk on By

Lyric by Hal David
Music by Burt Bacharach

F Harp 1st Position

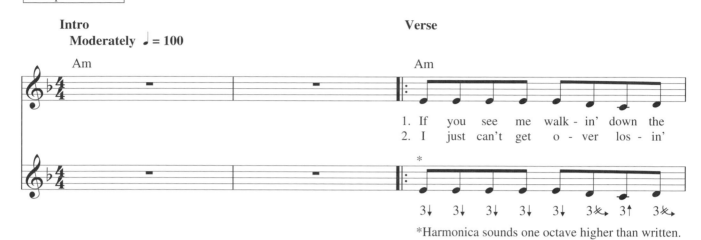

*Harmonica sounds one octave higher than written.

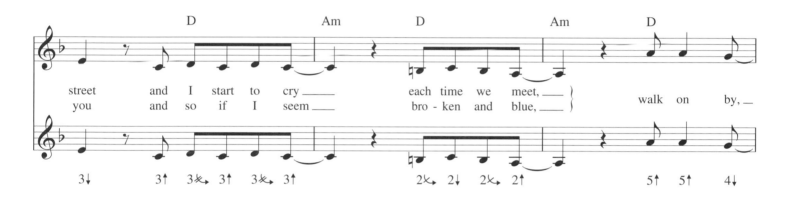

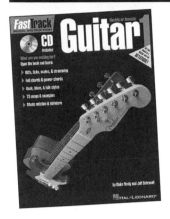

FastTrack MUSIC INSTRUCTION ®

*Fast*Track is the fastest way for beginners to learn to play the instrument they just bought. *Fast*Track is different from other method books: we've made our book/CD packs user-friendly with plenty of cool songs that make it easy and fun for players to teach themselves. Plus, the last section of the *Fast*Track books have the same songs so that students can form a band and jam together. Songbooks for Guitar, Bass, Keyboard and Drums are all compatible, and feature eight songs including hits such as Wild Thing • Twist and Shout • Layla • Born to Be Wild • and more! All packs include a great play-along CD with a professional-sounding back-up band.

FASTTRACK GUITAR

For Electric or Acoustic Guitar – or both!
by Blake Neely & Jeff Schroedl
Book/CD Packs

Teaches music notation, tablature, full chords and power chords, riffs, licks, scales, and rock and blues styles. Method Book 1 includes 73 songs and examples.

LEVEL 1
00697282 Method Book – 9" x 12" $7.95
00695390 Method Book – 5½" x 5" $7.95
00697287 Songbook 1 – 9" x 12" $12.95
00695397 Songbook 1 – 5½" x 5" $9.95
00695343 Songbook 2 ....$12.95
00696057 DVD..$7.99

LEVEL 2
00697286 Method Book......................................$9.95
00697296 Songbook 1 ....$12.95
00695344 Songbook 2 ....$12.95

CHORDS & SCALES
00697291 9" x 12"...$9.95
00695510 5½" x 5" $9.95

FASTTRACK BASS

by Blake Neely & Jeff Schroedl
Book/CD Packs

Everything you need to know about playing the bass, including music notation, tablature, riffs, licks, scales, syncopation, and rock and blues styles. Method Book 1 includes 75 songs and examples.

LEVEL 1
00697284 Method Book – 9" x 12" $7.95
00695395 Method Book – 5½" x 5" $7.95
00697289 Songbook 1 – 9" x 12" $12.95
00695400 Songbook 1 – 5½" x 5" $9.95
00695368 Songbook 2 ....$12.95
00696058 DVD..$7.99

LEVEL 2
00697294 Method Book......................................$9.95
00697298 Songbook 1 ....$12.95
00695369 Songbook 2 ....$12.95

FASTTRACK KEYBOARD

For Electric Keyboard, Synthesizer, or Piano
by Blake Neely & Gary Meisner
Book/CD Packs

Learn how to play that piano today! With this book you'll learn music notation, chords, riffs, licks, scales, syncopation, and rock and blues styles. Method Book 1 includes over 87 songs and examples.

LEVEL 1
00697283 Method Book – 9" x 12" $7.99
00695391 Method Book – 5½" x 5" $7.95
00697288 Songbook 1 – 9" x 12" $12.95
00695398 Songbook 1 – 5½" x 5" $9.95
00695366 Songbook 2 ....$12.95
00696060 DVD..$7.99

LEVEL 2
00697293 Method Book......................................$9.95
00697297 Songbook 1 ....$12.95
00695370 Songbook 2 ....$12.95

CHORDS & SCALES
00697292 9" x 12"...$9.95
00695511 5½" x 5" $9.95

FASTTRACK DRUM

by Blake Neely & Rick Mattingly
Book/CD Packs

With this book, you'll learn music notation, riffs and licks, syncopation, rock, blues and funk styles, and improvisation. Method Book 1 includes over 75 songs and examples.

LEVEL 1
00697285 Method Book – 9" x 12" $7.95
00695396 Method Book – 5½" x 5" $7.95
00697290 Songbook 1 – 9" x 12" $12.95
00695399 Songbook 1 – 5½" x 5" $9.95
00695367 Songbook 2 ....$12.95

LEVEL 2
00697295 Method Book......................................$9.95
00697299 Songbook 1 ....$12.95
00695371 Songbook 2 ....$12.95
00696059 DVD..$7.99

FASTTRACK SAXOPHONE

by Blake Neely
Book/CD Packs

With this book, you'll learn music notation; riffs, scales, keys; syncopation; rock and blues styles; and more. Includes 72 songs and examples.

LEVEL 1
00695241 Method Book...$7.95
00695409 Songbook...$12.95

FASTTRACK HARMONICA

by Blake Neely & Doug Downing
Book/CD Packs

These books cover all you need to learn C Diatonic harmonica, including: music notation • singles notes and chords • riffs, licks & scales • syncopation • rock and blues styles. Method Book 1 includes over 70 songs and examples.

LEVEL 1
00695407 Method Book...$7.95
00695574 Songbook...$12.95

LEVEL 2
00695889 Method Book...$9.95

FASTTRACK LEAD SINGER

by Blake Neely
Book/CD Packs

Everything you need to be a great singer, including: how to read music, microphone tips, warm-up exercises, ear training, syncopation, and more. Method Book 1 includes 80 songs and examples.

LEVEL 1
00695408 Method Book...$7.95
00695410 Songbook...$12.95

LEVEL 2
00695892 Songbook 1 ....$12.95

FOR MORE INFORMATION, SEE YOUR LOCAL MUSIC DEALER,
OR WRITE TO:

7777 W. BLUEMOUND RD. P.O. BOX 13819 MILWAUKEE, WI 53213

Prices, contents, and availability subject to change without notice. Some products may not be available outside the U.S.A.

Visit Hal Leonard online at **www.halleonard.com**

1109

THE HAL LEONARD HARMONICA METHOD AND SONGBOOKS

THE METHOD

THE HAL LEONARD COMPLETE HARMONICA METHOD – CHROMATIC HARMONICA

by Bobby Joe Holman

The only harmonica method to present the chromatic harmonica in 14 scales and modes in all 12 keys! This book/CD pack will take beginners from the basics on through to the most advanced techniques available for the contemporary harmonica player. Each section contains appropriate songs and exercises (which are demonstrated on the CD) that enable the player to quickly learn the various concepts presented. Every aspect of this versatile musical instrument is explored and explained in easy-to-understand detail with illustrations. The musical styles covered include traditional, blues, pop and rock.

_____00841286 Book/CD Pack $12.95

THE HAL LEONARD COMPLETE HARMONICA METHOD – DIATONIC HARMONICA

by Bobby Joe Holman

The only harmonica method specific to the diatonic harmonica, covering all six positions. This book/CD pack contains over 20 songs and musical examples that take beginners from the basics on through to the most advanced techniques available for the contemporary harmonica player. Each section contains appropriate songs and exercises (which are demonstrated on the CD) that enable the player to quickly learn the various concepts presented. Every aspect of this versatile musical instrument is explored and explained in easy-to-understand detail with illustrations. The musical styles covered include traditional, blues, pop and rock.

_____00841285 Book/CD Pack $12.95

Prices, contents and availability
subject to change without notice.

THE SONGBOOKS

The Hal Leonard Harmonica Songbook series offers a wide variety of music especially tailored to the two-volume Hal Leonard Harmonica Method, but can be played by all harmonica players, diatonic and chromatic alike. All books include study and performance notes, and a guide to harmonica tablature. From classical themes to Christmas music, rock and roll to Broadway, there's something for everyone!

BROADWAY SONGS FOR HARMONICA — INCLUDES TAB

arranged by Bobby Joe Holman

19 show-stopping Broadway tunes for the harmonica. Songs include: Ain't Misbehavin' • Bali Ha'i • Camelot • Climb Ev'ry Mountain • Do-Re-Mi • Edelweiss • Give My Regards to Broadway • Hello, Dolly! • I've Grown Accustomed to Her Face • The Impossible Dream (The Quest) • Memory • Oklahoma • People • and more.

_____00820009 ....$9.95

CHRISTMAS CAROLS & HYMNS FOR HARMONICA — INCLUDES TAB

arranged by Bobby Joe Holman

This book features 19 holiday songs for diatonic and chromatic harmonicas: Auld Lang Syne • Away in a Manger • Deck the Hall • The First Noel • Jingle Bells • Joy to the World • O Little Town of Bethlehem • Silent Night • What Child Is This? • more. Includes study and performance notes, and a guide to harmonica tablature.

_____00820008 ....$9.95

CLASSICAL FAVORITES FOR HARMONICA — INCLUDES TAB

arranged by Bobby Joe Holman

18 famous classical melodies and themes, arranged for diatonic and chromatic players. Includes: By the Beautiful Blue Danube • Clair De Lune • The Flight of the Bumble Bee • Gypsy Rondo • Moonlight Sonata • Surprise Symphony • The Swan (Le Cygne) • Waltz of the Flowers • and more, plus a guide to harmonica tablature.

_____00820006 ....$9.95

MOVIE FAVORITES FOR HARMONICA — INCLUDES TAB

arranged by Bobby Joe Holman

19 songs from the silver screen, arranged for diatonic and chromatic harmonica. Includes: Alfie • Bless the Beasts and Children • Chim Chim Cher-ee • The Entertainer • Georgy Girl • Midnight Cowboy • Moon River • Picnic • Speak Softly, Love • Stormy Weather • Tenderly • Unchained Melody • What a Wonderful World • and more, plus a guide to harmonica tablature.

_____00820014 ....$9.95

POP ROCK FAVORITES FOR HARMONICA — INCLUDES TAB

arranged by Bobby Joe Holman

17 classic hits especially arranged for harmonica (either diatonic or chromatic), including: Abraham, Martin and John • All I Have to Do Is Dream • Blueberry Hill • Daydream • Runaway • Sixteen Candles • Sleepwalk • Something • Stand by Me • Tears on My Pillow • Tell It like It Is • Yakety Yak • and more.

_____00820013 ....$9.95

TV FAVORITES FOR HARMONICA — INCLUDES TAB

arranged by Bobby Joe Holman

21 top tube tunes arranged for diatonic and chromatic harmonica: The Ballad of Davy Crockett • Theme from Beauty and the Beast • Theme from Bewitched • The Brady Bunch • Bubbles in the Wine • Father Knows Best Theme • Hands of Time • Happy Days • The Little House (On the Prairie) • Nadia's Theme • The Odd Couple • Twin Peaks Theme • Theme from The Untouchables • Victory at Sea • William Tell Overture • Wings • and more.

_____00820007 ....$9.95

FOR MORE INFORMATION, SEE YOUR LOCAL MUSIC DEALER,
OR WRITE TO:

HAL•LEONARD® CORPORATION

7777 W. BLUEMOUND RD. P.O. BOX 13819 MILWAUKEE, WI 53213

Visit Hal Leonard Online at
www.halleonard.com

1108